INTERMEDIATE PIANO DUETS / 1 PIANO, 4 HANDS

Christmas at the Piano

ISBN 978-0-634-01922-7

HAL•LEONARD®
CORPORATION
7777 W. BLUEMOUND RD. P.O. BOX 13819 MILWAUKEE, WI 53213

Visit Hal Leonard Online at
www.halleonard.com

Christmas at the Piano

CAROLING, CAROLING

SECONDO

Words by WIHLA HUTSON
Music by ALFRED BURT

With a lilt

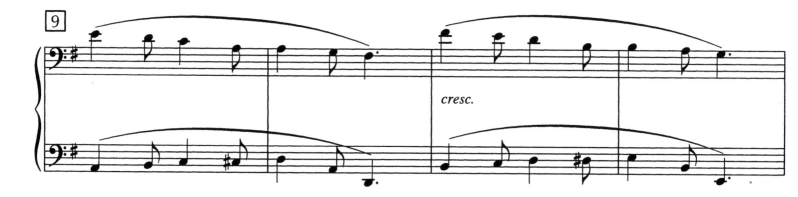

CAROLING, CAROLING

PRIMO

Words by WIHLA HUTSON
Music by ALFRED BURT

SECONDO

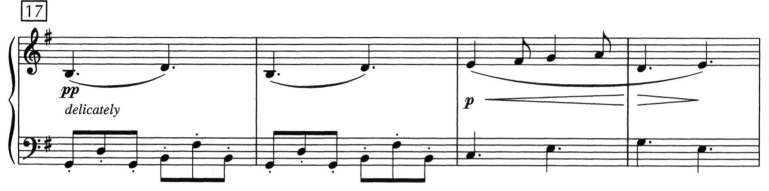

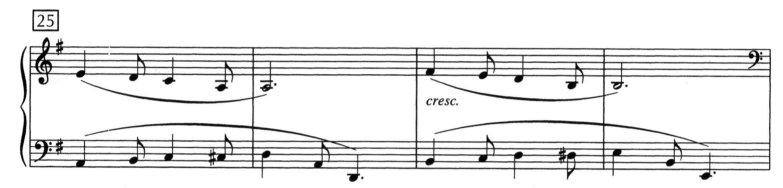

PRIMO

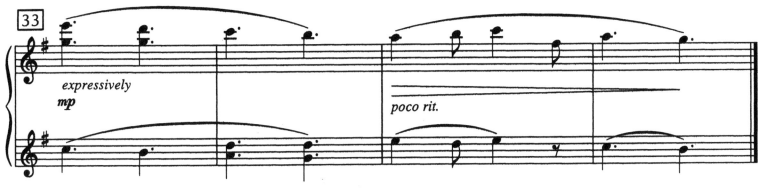

DO YOU HEAR WHAT I HEAR

SECONDO

Words and Music by
NOEL REGNEY and GLORIA SHAYNE

Moderately

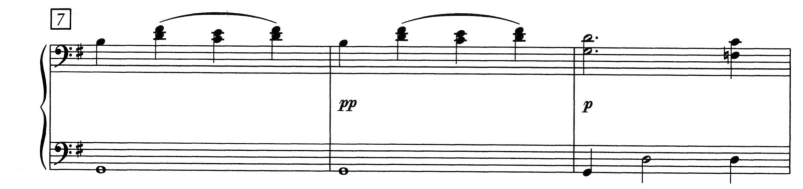

DO YOU HEAR WHAT I HEAR

PRIMO

Words and Music by
NOEL REGNEY and GLORIA SHAYNE

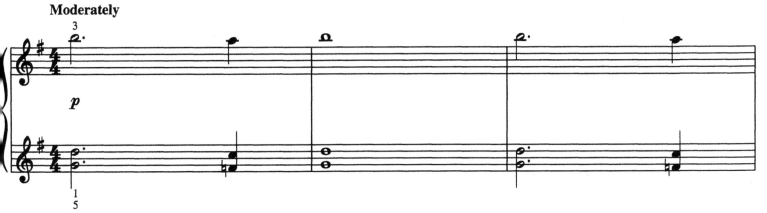

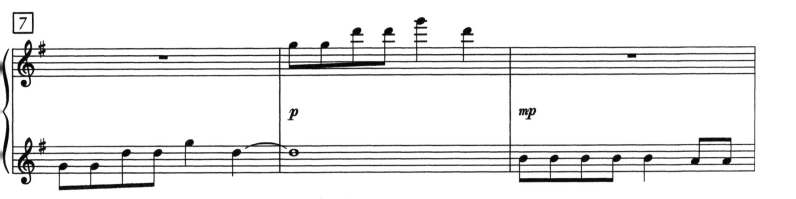

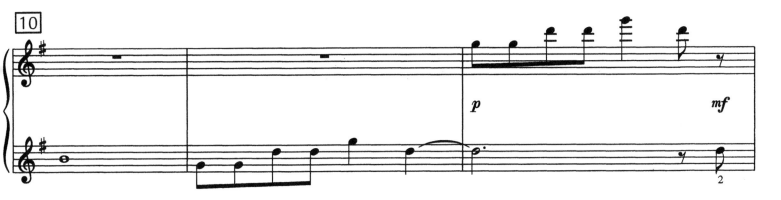

SECONDO

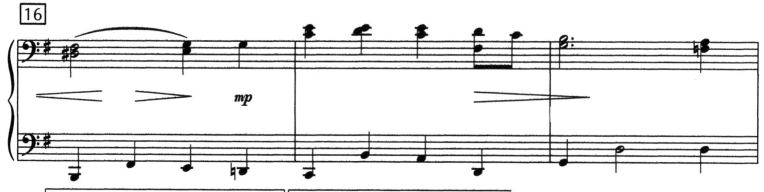

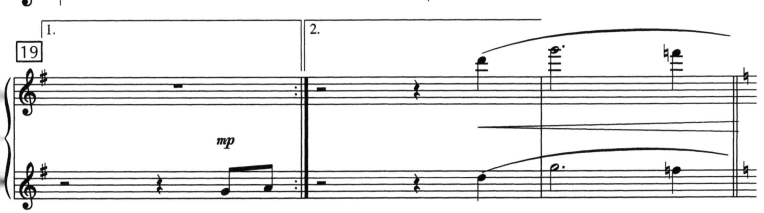

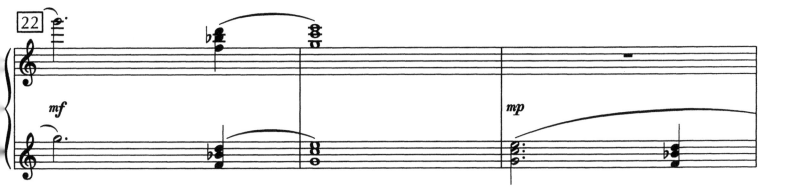

SECONDO

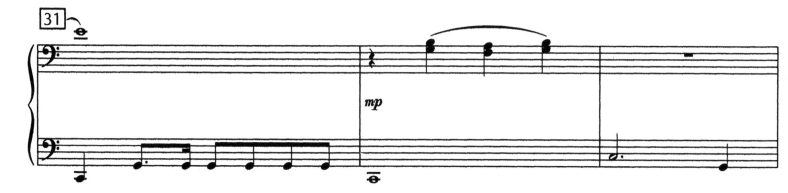

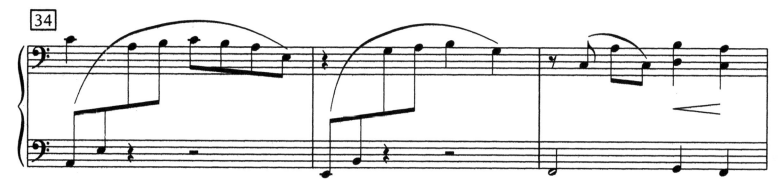

PRIMO

HAPPY HOLIDAY

from the Motion Picture Irving Berlin's HOLIDAY INN

SECONDO

Words and Music by
IRVING BERLIN

Moderately, with a bounce

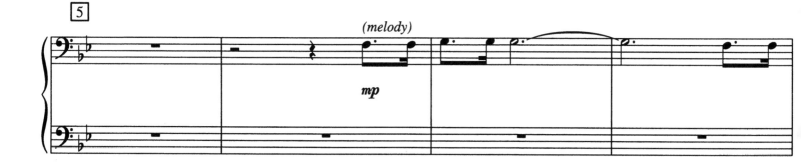

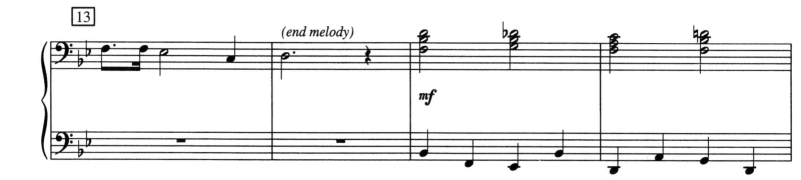

HAPPY HOLIDAY

from the Motion Picture Irving Berlin's HOLIDAY INN

PRIMO

Words and Music by
IRVING BERLIN

Moderately, with a bounce

SECONDO

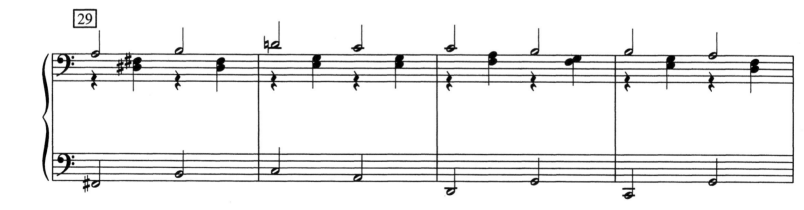

PRIMO

SECONDO

PRIMO

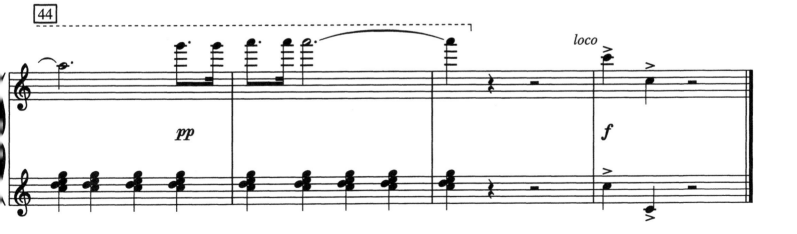

HAPPY XMAS
(WAR IS OVER)

SECONDO

Words and Music by JOHN LENNON
and YOKO ONO

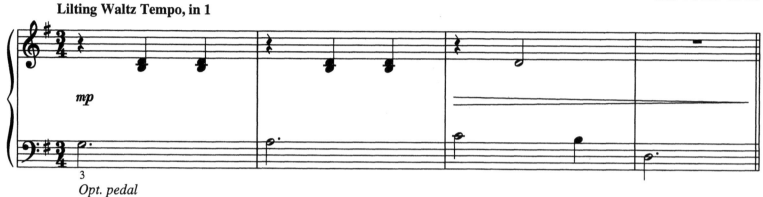

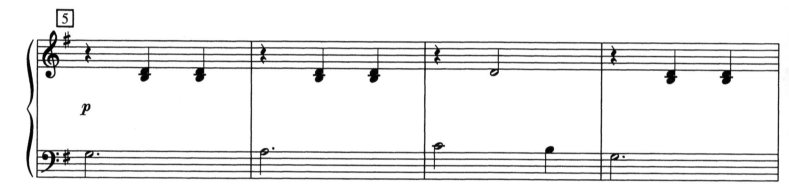

HAPPY XMAS
(WAR IS OVER)

PRIMO

Words and Music by JOHN LENNON
and YOKO ONO

Lilting Waltz Tempo, in 1

Opt. pedal

SECONDO

PRIMO

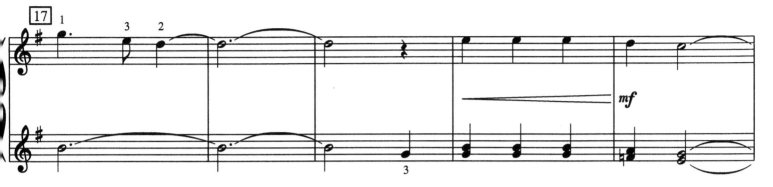

SECONDO

(Melody)

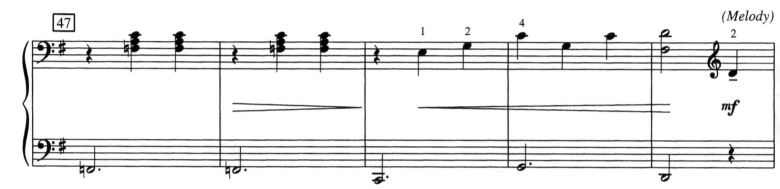

(end melody)

PRIMO

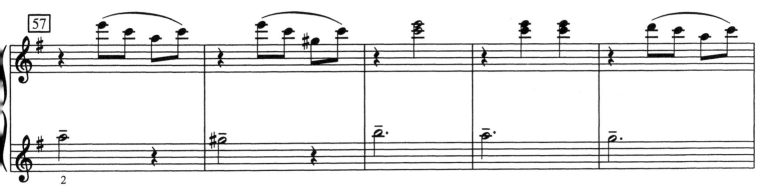

26

SECONDO

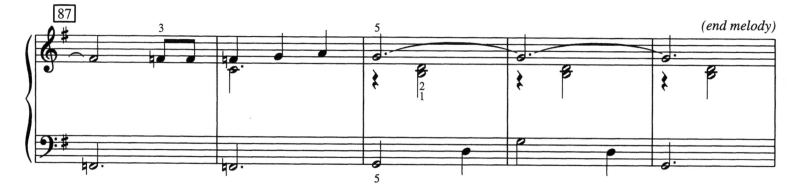

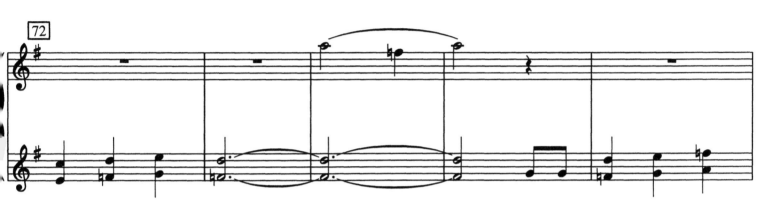

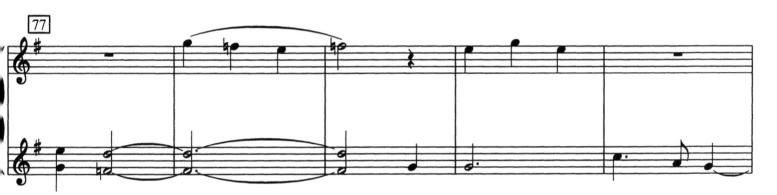

SECONDO

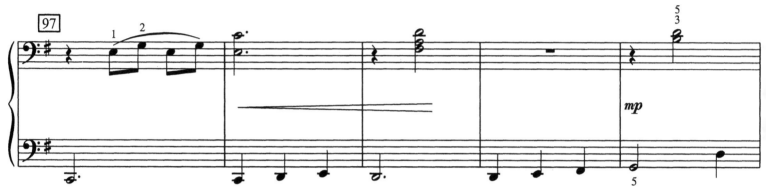

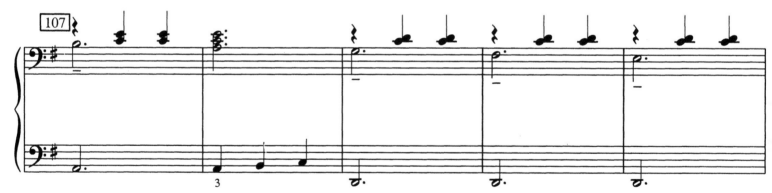

PRIMO

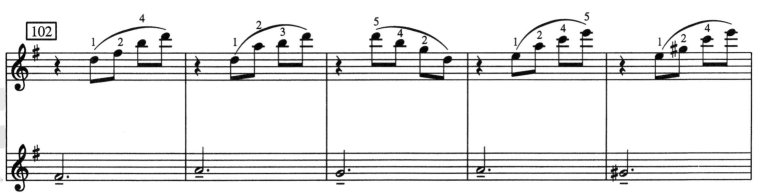

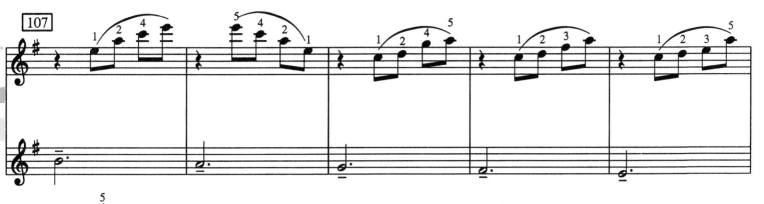

rit. poco a poco   *espressivo*

I HEARD THE BELLS ON CHRISTMAS DAY

SECONDO

Words by HENRY WADSWORTH LONGFELLOW
Adapted by JOHNNY MARKS
Music by JOHNNY MARKS

Moderately slow

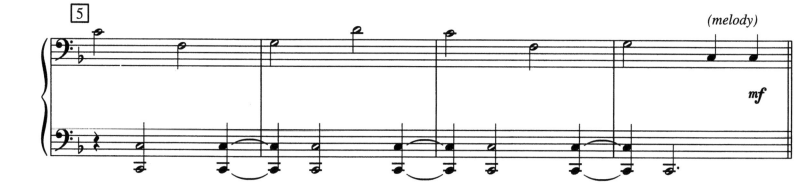

I HEARD THE BELLS ON CHRISTMAS DAY

PRIMO

Words by HENRY WADSWORTH LONGFELLOW
Adapted by JOHNNY MARKS
Music by JOHNNY MARKS

SECONDO

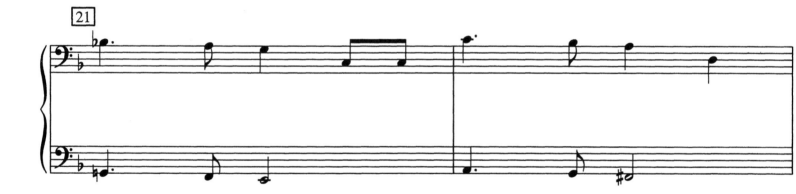

PRIMO

SECONDO

PRIMO

SECONDO

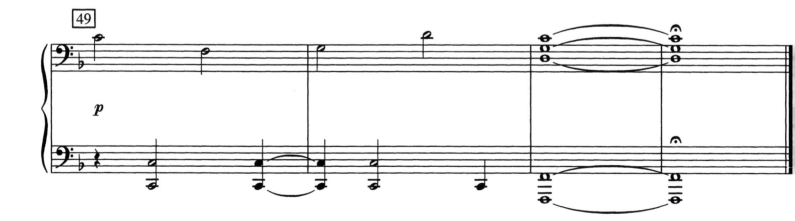

PRIMO

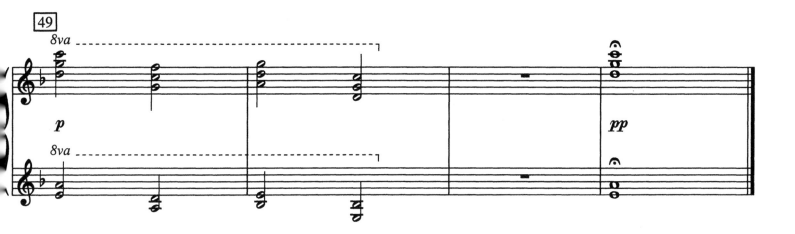

I SAW MOMMY KISSING SANTA CLAUS

SECONDO

Words and Music by
TOMMIE CONNOR

Moderately

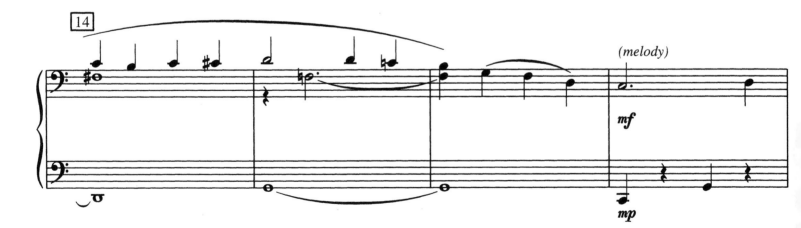

I SAW MOMMY KISSING SANTA CLAUS

PRIMO

Words and Music by
TOMMIE CONNOR

Moderately

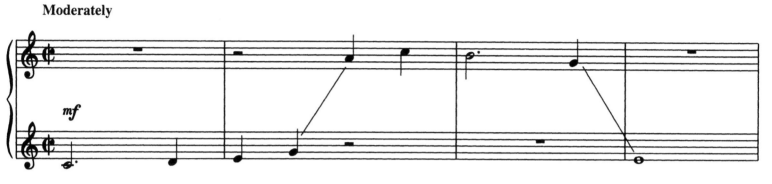

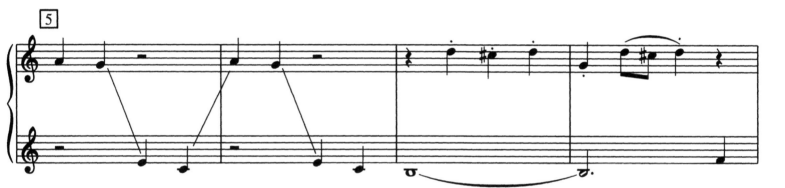

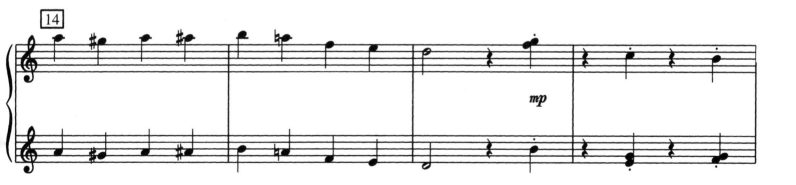

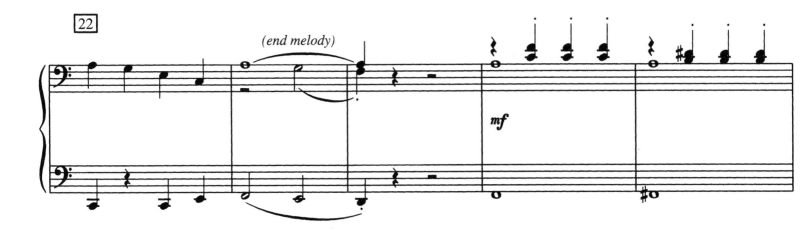

PRIMO

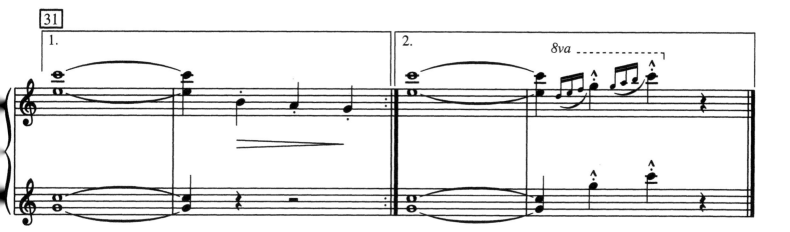

I'LL BE HOME FOR CHRISTMAS

SECONDO

Words and Music by
KIM GANNON and WALTER KENT

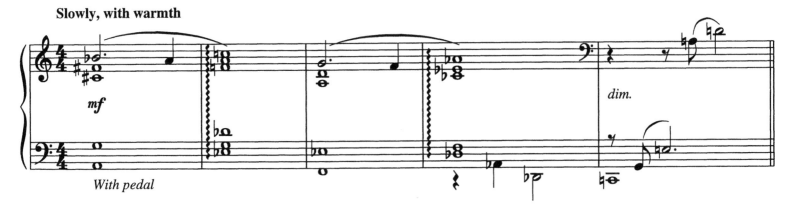

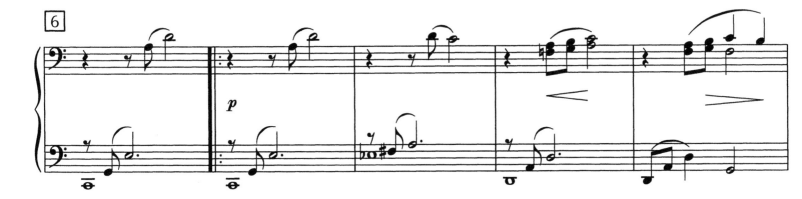

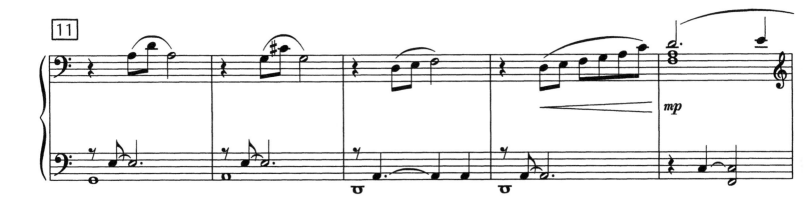

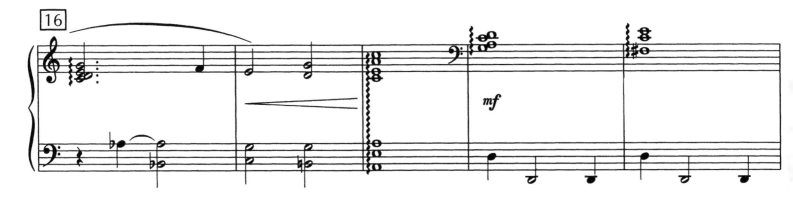

I'LL BE HOME FOR CHRISTMAS

PRIMO

Words and Music by
KIM GANNON and WALTER KENT

Slowly, with warmth

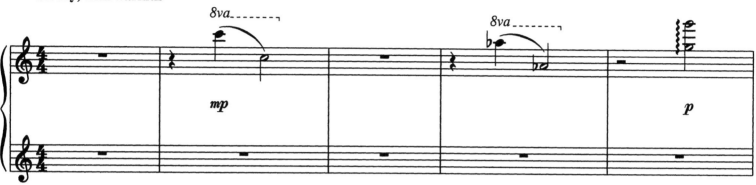

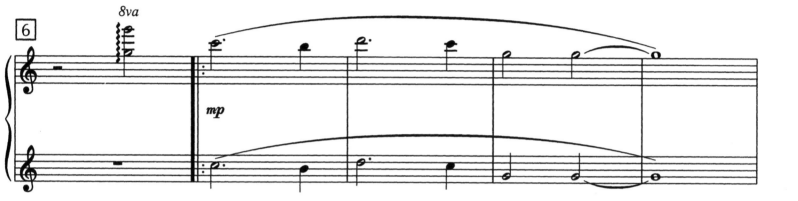

SECONDO

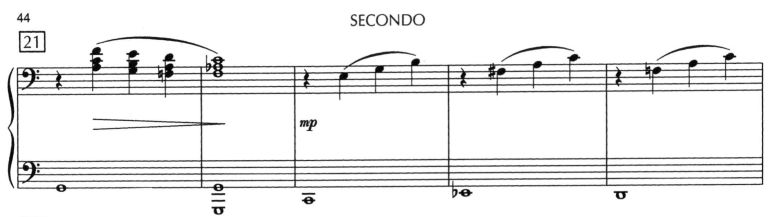

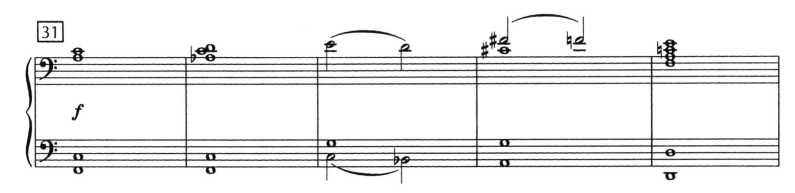

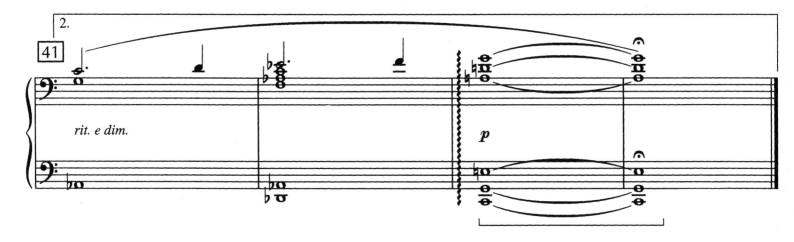

PRIMO

LAST CHRISTMAS

SECONDO

Words and Music by
GEORGE MICHAEL

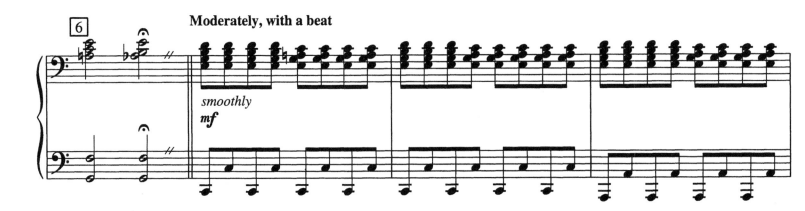

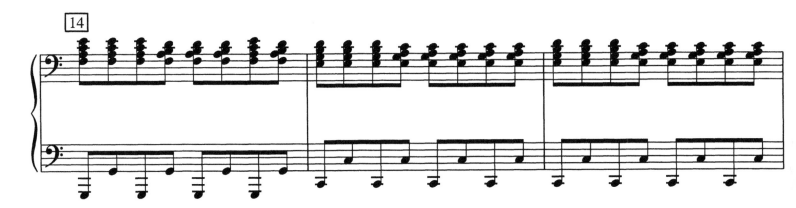

LAST CHRISTMAS

PRIMO

Words and Music by
GEORGE MICHAEL

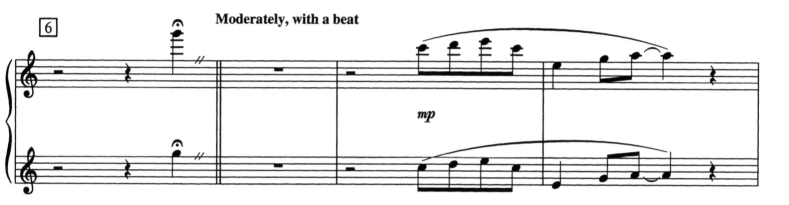

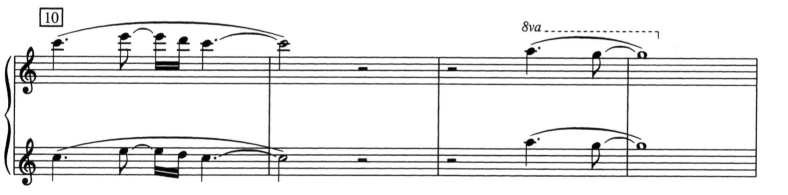

SECONDO

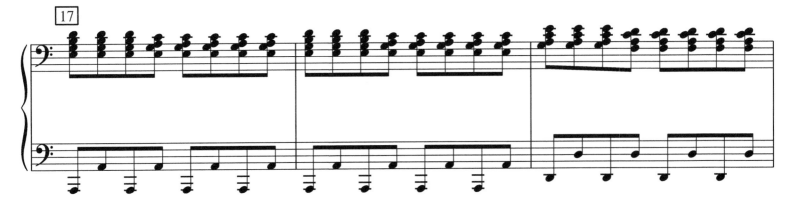

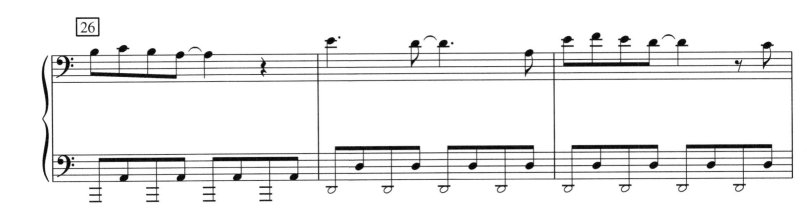

PRIMO

SECONDO

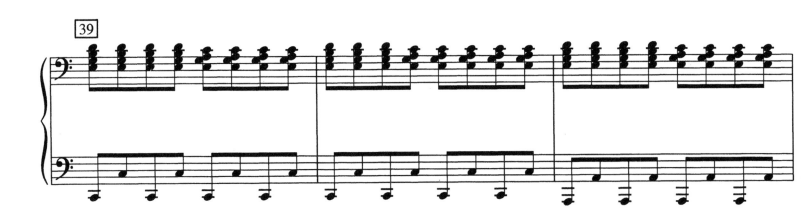

PRIMO

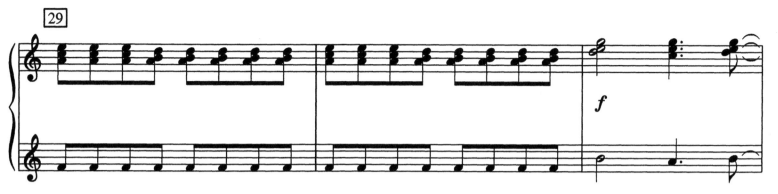

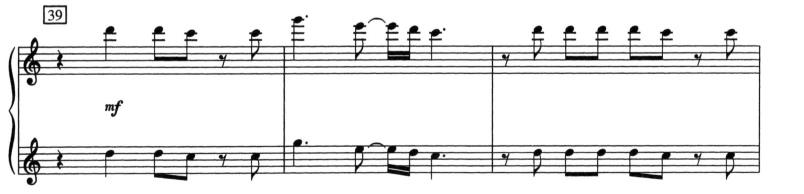

SECONDO

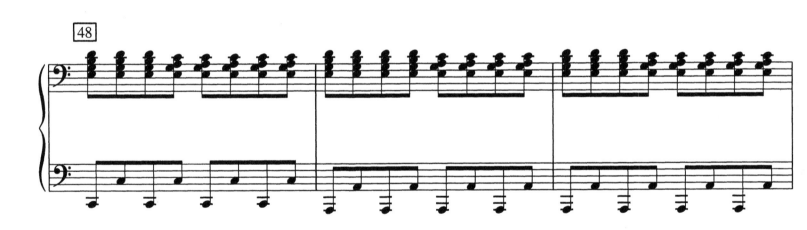

SECONDO

PRIMO

LET IT SNOW! LET IT SNOW! LET IT SNOW!

SECONDO

Words by SAMMY CAHN
Music by JULE STYNE

With a lilt; not too fast

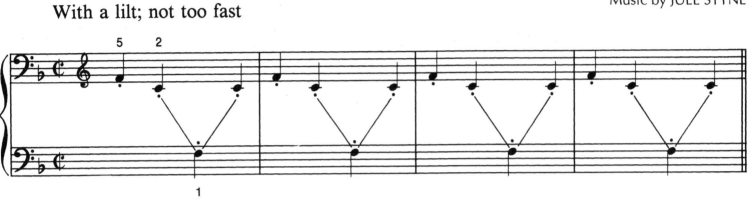

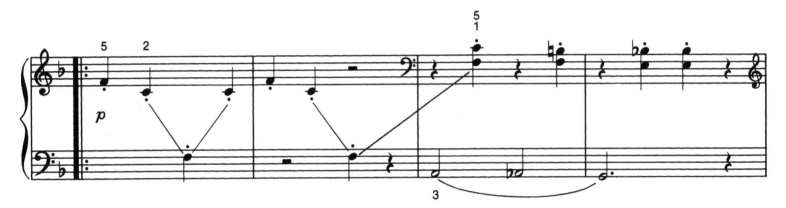

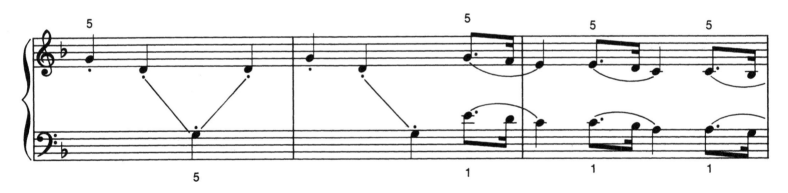

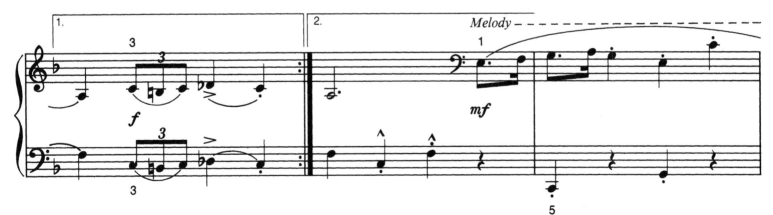

LET IT SNOW! LET IT SNOW! LET IT SNOW!

PRIMO

Words by SAMMY CAHN
Music by JULE STYNE

With a lilt, not too fast

SECONDO

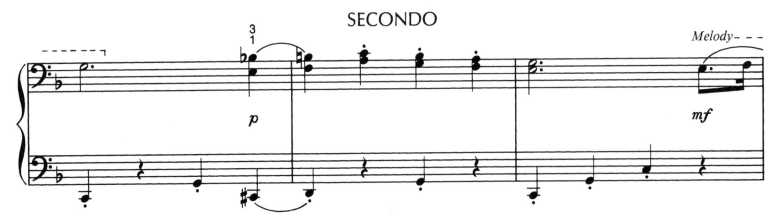

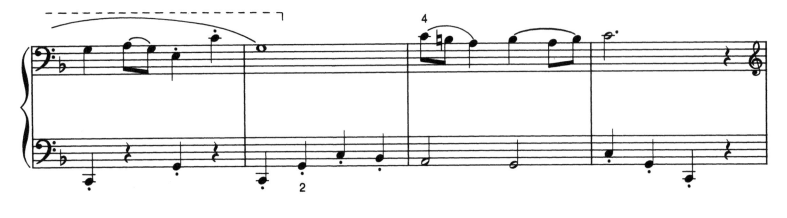

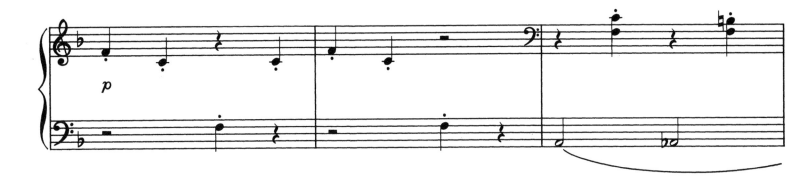

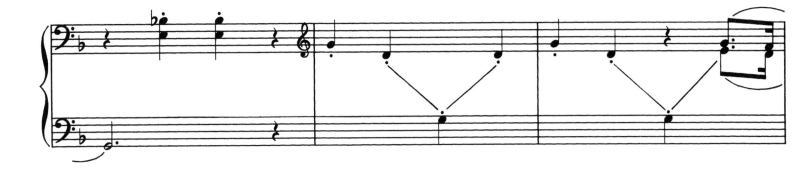

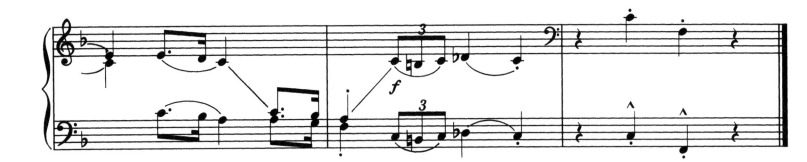

PRIMO

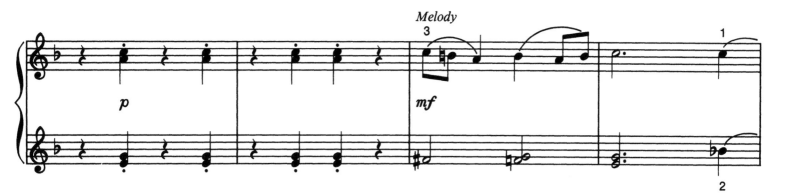

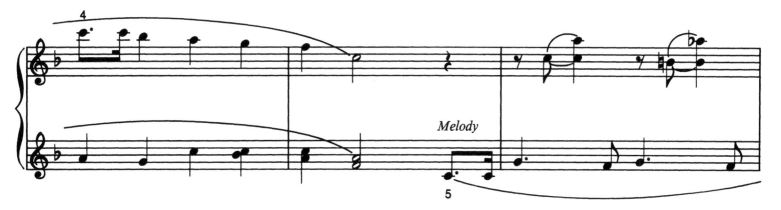

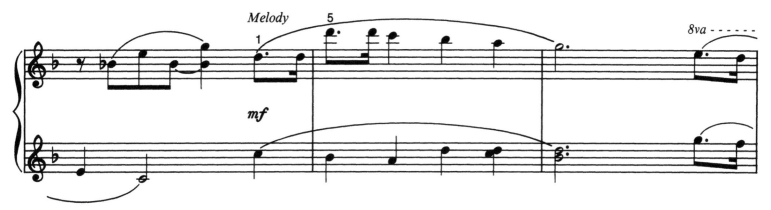

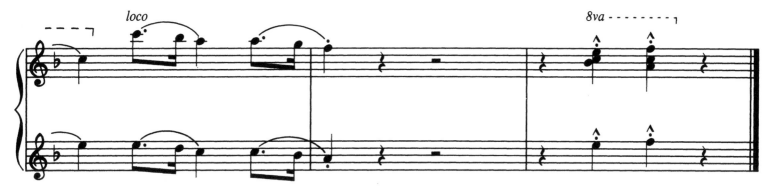

WHITE CHRISTMAS

from the Motion Picture Irving Berlin's HOLIDAY INN

SECONDO

Words and Music by
IRVING BERLIN

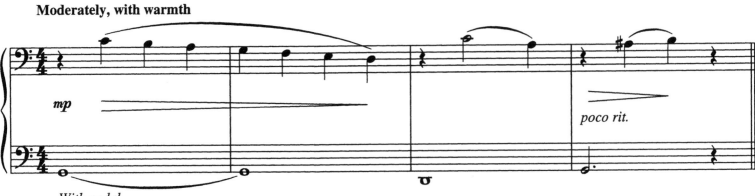

WHITE CHRISTMAS
from the Motion Picture Irving Berlin's HOLIDAY INN

PRIMO

Words and Music by
IRVING BERLIN

Moderately, with warmth

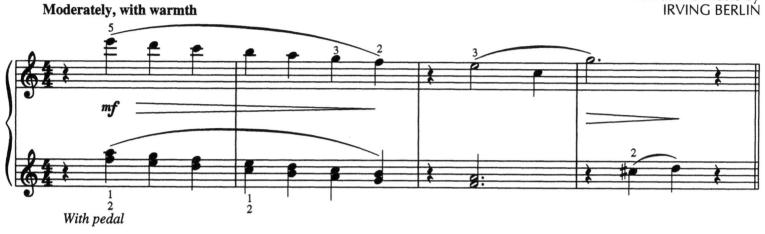

With pedal

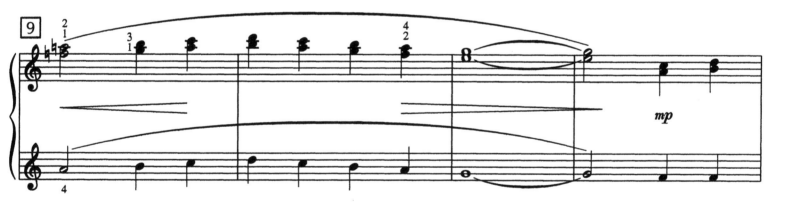

62

SECONDO

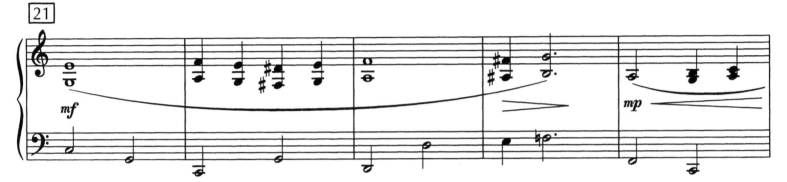

PRIMO

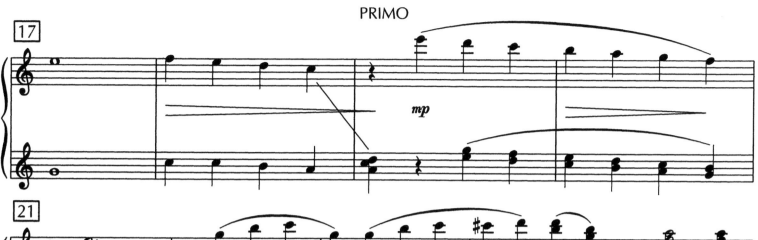

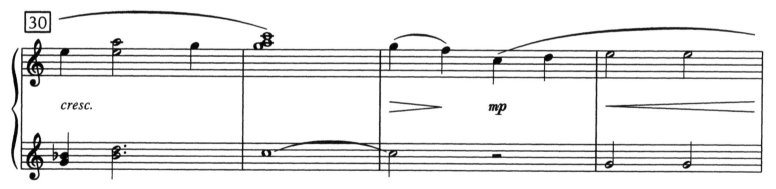

WONDERFUL CHRISTMASTIME

SECONDO

Words and Music by
McCARTNEY

WONDERFUL CHRISTMASTIME

PRIMO

Words and Music by
McCARTNEY

SECONDO

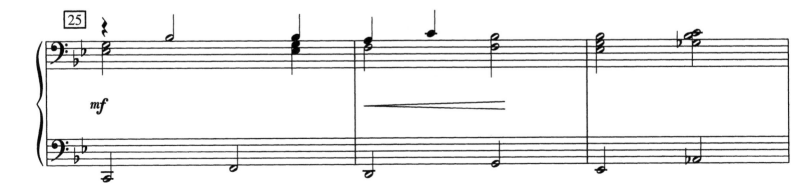

PRIMO

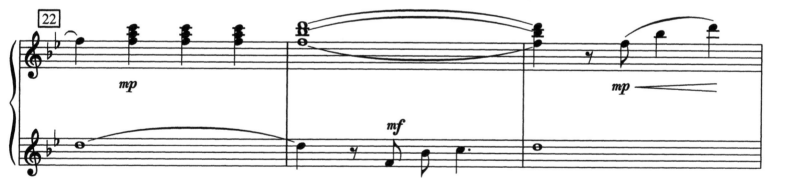

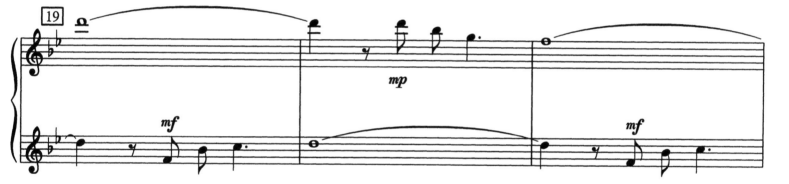

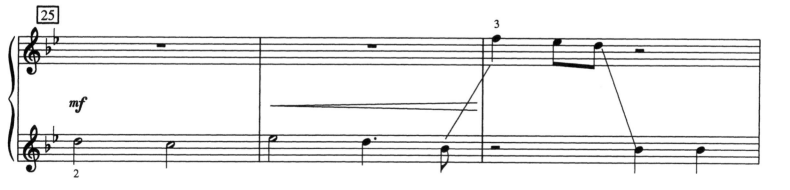

68

SECONDO

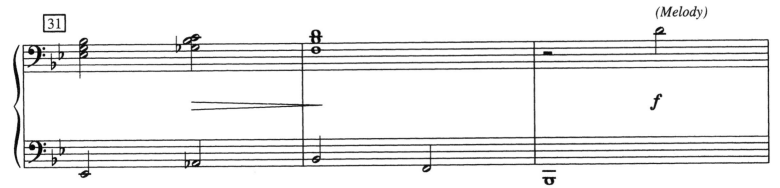

(Melody)

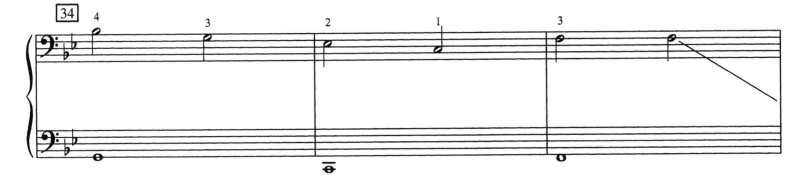

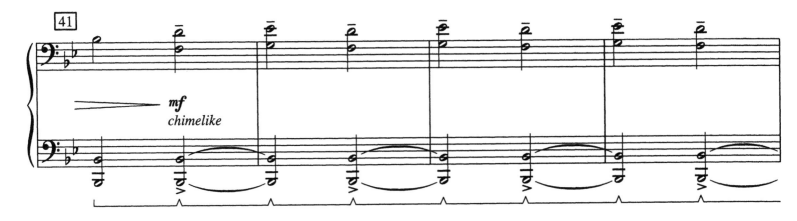

PRIMO

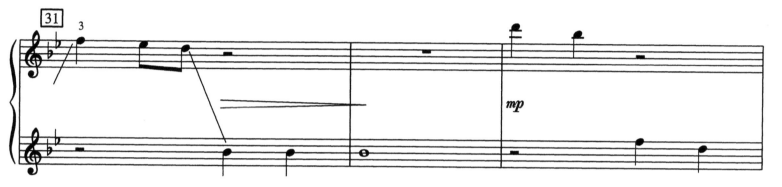

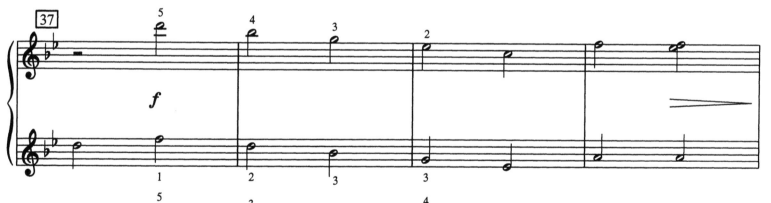

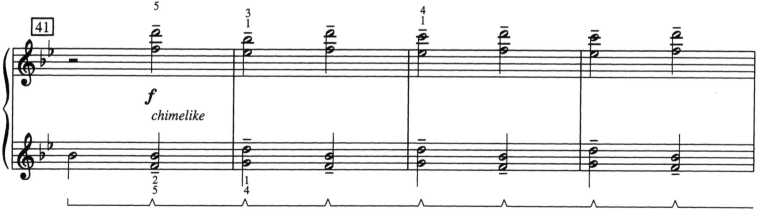

SECONDO

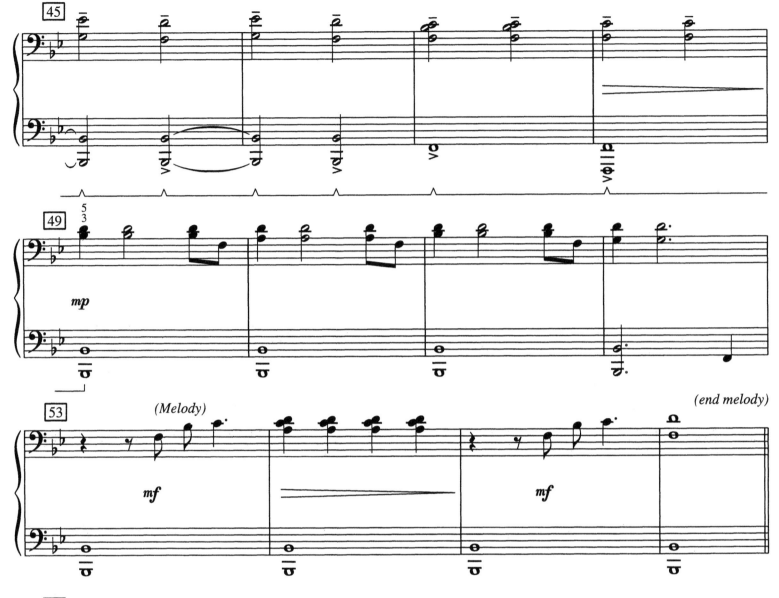

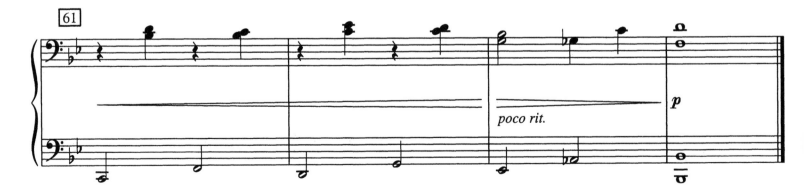

PRIMO

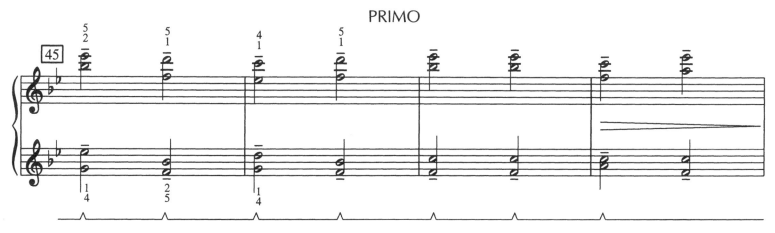

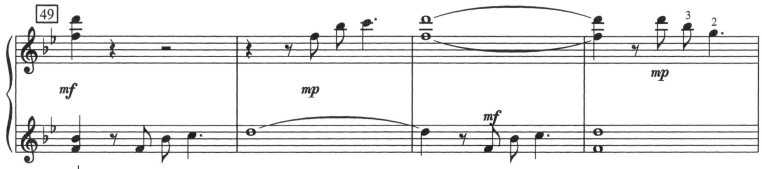

PIANO FOR TWO
A Variety of Piano Duets from Hal Leonard

ADELE FOR PIANO DUET
Intermediate Level

Eight of Adele's biggest hits arranged especially for intermediate piano duet! Featuring: Chasing Pavements • Hello • Make You Feel My Love • Rolling in the Deep • Set Fire to the Rain • Skyfall • Someone Like You • When We Were Young.
00172162 1 Piano, 4 Hands................................$14.99

THE BEATLES FOR PIANO DUET
Intermediate Level
arr. Eric Baumgartner

Eight great Beatles' songs arranged for piano duet! Titles: Blackbird • Come Together • In My Life • Lucy in the Sky with Diamonds • Michelle • Ob-la-di, Ob-la-da • While My Guitar Gently Weeps • Yellow Submarine.
00275877 1 Piano, 4 Hands $14.99

THE BIG BOOK OF PIANO DUETS

24 great piano duet arrangements! Includes: Beauty and the Beast • Clocks • Edelweiss • Georgia on My Mind • He's a Pirate • Let It Go • Linus and Lucy • Moon River • Yellow Submarine • You are the Sunshine of My Life • and more!
00232851 1 Piano, 4 Hands...............................$17.99

CONTEMPORARY DISNEY DUETS
Intermediate Level

8 great Disney duets: Evermore (from Beauty and the Beast) • How Does a Moment Last Forever (from Beauty and the Beast) • How Far I'll Go (from Moana) • Lava • Let It Go (from Frozen) • Proud Corazon (from Coco) • Remember Me (from Coco) • You're Welcome (from Moana).
00285562 1 Piano, 4 Hands...............................$12.99

EASY CLASSICAL DUETS
Book/Online Audio
Willis Music

7 great piano duets to perform at a recital, play-for-fun, or sightread: By the Beautiful Blue Danube (Strauss) • Eine kleine Nachtmusik (Mozart) • Hungarian Rhapsody No. 5 (Liszt) • Morning from Peer Gynt (Grieg) • Rondeau (Mouret) • Sleeping Beauty Waltz (Tchaikovsky) • Surprise Symphony (Haydn). Includes online audio tracks for the primo and secondo part for download or streaming.
00145767 1 Piano, 4 Hands $12.99

FAVORITE DISNEY SONGS FOR PIANO DUET
Early Intermediate Level

8 great Disney songs creatively arranged for piano duet: Can You Feel the Love Tonight • Do You Want to Build a Snowman • A Dream Is a Wish Your Heart Makes • Supercalifragilisticexpialidocious • That's How You Know • When Will My Life Begin? • You'll Be in My Heart • You've Got a Friend in Me.
00285563 1 Piano, 4 Hands..............................$14.99

FIRST 50 PIANO DUETS YOU SHOULD PLAY

Includes: Autumn Leaves • Bridge over Troubled Water • Chopsticks • Fields of Gold • Hallelujah • Imagine • Lean on Me • Theme from "New York, New York" • Over the Rainbow • Peaceful Easy Feeling • Singin' in the Rain • A Thousand Years • What the World Needs Now Is Love • You Raise Me Up • and more.
00276571 1 Piano, 4 Hands $24.99

GOSPEL DUETS
The Phillip Keveren Series

Eight inspiring hymns arranged by Phillip Keveren for one piano, four hands, including: Church in the Wildwood • His Eye Is on the Sparrow • In the Garden • Just a Closer Walk with Thee • The Old Rugged Cross • Shall We Gather at the River? • There Is Power in the Blood • When the Roll Is Called up Yonder.
00295099 1 Piano, 4 Hands.............................$12.99

THE GREATEST SHOWMAN
by Benj Pasek & Justin Paul
Intermediate Level

Creative piano duet arrangements for the songs: Come Alive • From Now On • The Greatest Show • A Million Dreams • Never Enough • The Other Side • Rewrite the Stars • This Is Me • Tightrope.
00295078 1 Piano, 4 Hands.............................$16.99

BILLY JOEL FOR PIANO DUET
Intermediate Level

8 of the Piano Man's greatest hits – perfect as recital encores, or just for fun! Titles: It's Still Rock and Roll to Me • Just the Way You Are • The Longest Time • My Life • New York State of Mind • Piano Man • She's Always a Woman • Uptown Girl.
00141139 1 Piano, 4 Hands $14.99

HEART AND SOUL & OTHER DUET FAVORITES

8 fun duets arranged for two people playing on one piano. Includes: Any Dream Will Do • Chopsticks • Heart and Soul • Music! Music! Music! (Put Another Nickel In) • On Top of Spaghetti • Raiders March • The Rainbow Connection • Y.M.C.A..
00290541 1 Piano, 4 Hands $12.99

RHAPSODY IN BLUE
George Gershwin/ arr. Brent Edstrom

Originally written for piano and jazz band, "Rhapsody in Blue" was later orchestrated by Ferde Grofe. This intimate adaptation for piano duet delivers access to advancing pianists and provides an exciting musical collaboration and adventure!
00125150 1 Piano, 4 Hands $14.99

RIVER FLOWS IN YOU & OTHER SONGS FOR PIANO DUET
Intermediate Level

10 great songs including the title song and: All of Me (Piano Guys) • Bella's Lullaby • Beyond • Chariots of Fire • Dawn • Forrest Gump - Main Title (Feather Theme) • Primavera • Somewhere in Time • Watermark.
00141055 1 Piano, 4 Hands $12.99

TOP HITS FOR EASY PIANO DUET
 Book/Online Audio
arr. David Pearl

10 great songs with backing tracks: Despacito (Justin Bieber ft. Luis Fonsi & Daddy Yankee) • Havana (Camila Cabello ft. Young Thug • High Hopes (Panic! At the Disco) • A Million Dreams (*The Greatest Showman*) • Perfect (Ed Sheeran) • Senorita (Camila Cabello & Shawn Mendes) • Shallow (Lady Gaga & Bradley Cooper) • Someone You Loved (Lewis Capaldi) • Speechless (*Aladdin*) • Sucker (Jonas Brothers).
00326133 1 Piano, 4 Hands..............................$12.99

HAL•LEONARD®
www.halleonard.com

0722
054